KB244181

Amazing Animals of the Amazon

About Wise & Wide

- A systematic 6-level English reading program based on Lexile® measures
- Diverse and interesting topics chosen from the elementary curriculums of Korea and English speaking western countries
- Well-written books in various forms including fiction stories, descriptive texts, and classics retold
- The informative but original fiction stories grab your interest, leading to the easy and clear understanding of the educational content.
- Improve thinking skills with solid after-reading activities at all levels of the series.

Wise & Wide is a 6-level English reading program that consists of 60 books and each level is systematically divided by Lexile® measures. The Lexile® Framework for Reading is the most popular reading measuring system in American formal education curriculums and many English programs. Over 20 out of 50 states in the U.S. mark Lexile® measures directly on students' final report cards and over 300 well-known publishers adopt and use Lexile® measures.

Experience many kinds of readings written by professional writers from the U.S. and England. They used interesting topics that were carefully chosen after analyzing elementary curriculums from around the world including Korea, the U.S., England, and Australia among many others. Comprehensive after-reading activities including graphic organizers, speaking tasks, and After-reading Tests are ready for you.

Levels in the series and their corresponding Lexile® measures

Level	Lexile® measures	U.S. Grade
Level 1	Below 200L	Pre K - K
Level 2	190L - 400L	Lower Grade 1
Level 3	350L - 530L	Upper Grade 1
Level 4	420L - 650L	Grade 2
Level 5	520L - 940L	Grade 3 - 4
Level 6	830L - 1070L	Grade 5 - 6

* Smart Readers: Wise & Wide level 1 is applicable to the preschool level in the U.S.

* The source of the relationship between Lexile® measures and U.S. school grades: CCSS(Common Core State Standards) FOR ENGLISH LANGUAGE ARTS, APPENDIX A (2012, which is used by 45 states in the U.S.)

Topic List

	Level 1	Level 2	Level 3	Level 4	Level 5	Level 6
Book 1	Science>Biology: The hibernation of animals Story	Science>Biology: Living and nonliving things Story	Science>Biology> Animals & the Environment: Sea otters Story	Environment> Living with nature: The diver & the persimmon tree Story	Science>Biology> Animal: Amazing animals of the Amazon Story	Science>Biology: Germs, transmitted diseases Story
Book 2	Literature> World classics: Aesop's fables Story	Literature> Traditional fairy tale: Old tales about stones Story	Social Studies> Economy: To run a business to make and save money Story	Science>Biology> Plants: Photosynthesis Story	Science>Earth science: Earth's layers,earthquakes, volcanoes, and earth's atmosphere Report	Mathematics> Sequence: The golden ratio & the Fibonacci sequence Story
Book 3	Science>Physics: How shadows are formed Story	Literature> World classics: Peter Pan Story	Science>Scientific technology: Nanobots Story	Literature>Myths: World's creation stories Story	Literature> Legend: The story of King Arthur Story	
Book 4	Literature> Traditional literature: The Talmud Story	Science>Biology> Animal: Polar bears Story	Science>Biology> Animal: Mountain gorillas Story	Social Studies> Cultural anthropology: Amazing ancient cultures of the world Story	Science> Earth science: Clouds and weather Story	
Book 5			Social Studies> Cultural anthropology: Astonishing festivals Report	Art>Music: Stories from two operas Story		
Book 6				Social Studies> People: Three great people who overcame hardships Story		
Book 7						
Book 8						
Book 9						
Book 10						

* 10 books in each level will be published.

How to Use This Book

•Before Reading

You can easily find the topic and what kind of story you are about to read.

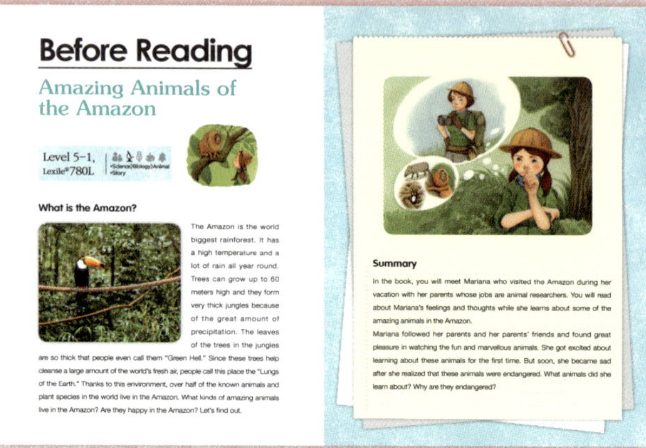

•The text

All the stories were written by professional writers from the U.S. and England, so you will read authentic and appropriate English sentences and expressions in every book in the series.

•Pop Quiz

Check out right away if you understand what you have just read by solving a pop quiz that checks your comprehension.

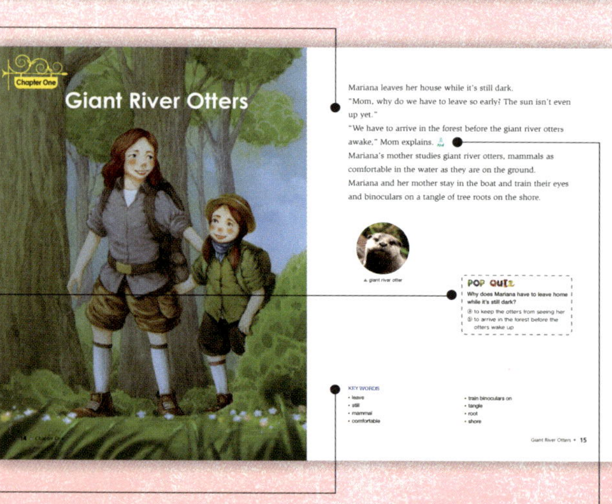

•Key Words

The key words and expressions on each page are listed for you to easily study them.

•Aha! Tips

Download free Korean explanations at *www.ihappyhouse.co.kr* for all of the sentences marked with "Aha!". These explain cultural, scientific, and economic knowledge or they deal with aspects of English such as grammatical structures or idiomatic expressions. There are lots of "Aha! Tips" to help you understand the text.

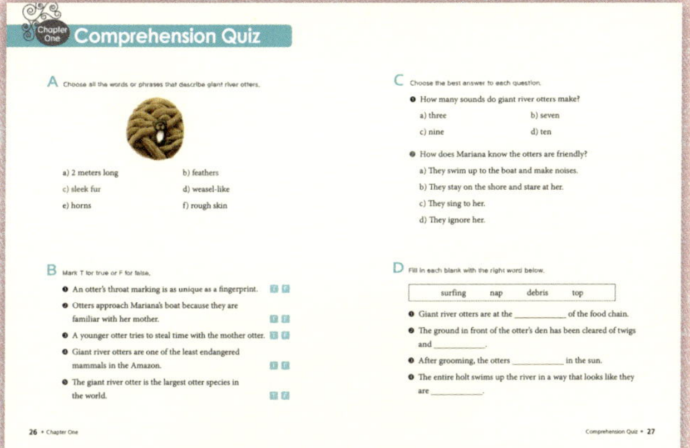

•Comprehension Quiz

After reading one chapter, solve various questions to find out if you fully understand the content.

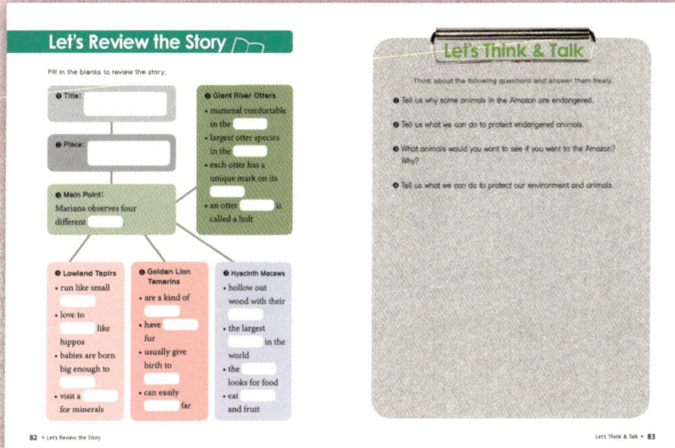

•Let's Review the Story /
•Let's Think & Talk

Fill in the blanks in the organizer to summarize the whole story. Express your own thinking and feelings about the story by answering the questions. You can build up logic and reasoning skills for your essay examinations in the future.

Appendix 

Audio CD
In the CD audio book form, the texts are read vividly by American professional voice actors.

After-reading Test
Solve an additionally provided After-reading Test for each book.

The Korean translation, Answer Keys, a Word Quiz, a Word List, and Aha! Tips for each book
You can download them for free at *www.ihappyhouse.co.kr*

Before Reading

Amazing Animals of the Amazon

Level 5–1,
Lexile® 780L

•Science〉Biology〉Animal
•Story

What is the Amazon?

The Amazon is the world biggest rainforest. It has a high temperature and a lot of rain all year round. Trees can grow up to 60 meters high and they form very thick jungles because of the great amount of precipitation. The leaves of the trees in the jungles are so thick that people even call them "Green Hell." Since these trees help cleanse a large amount of the world's fresh air, people call this place the "Lungs of the Earth." Thanks to this environment, over half of the known animals and plant species in the world live in the Amazon. What kinds of amazing animals live in the Amazon? Are they happy in the Amazon? Let's find out.

Summary

In the book, you will meet Mariana who visited the Amazon during her vacation with her parents whose jobs are animal researchers. You will read about Mariana's feelings and thoughts while she learns about some of the amazing animals in the Amazon.

Mariana followed her parents and her parents' friends and found great pleasure in watching the fun and marvellous animals. She got excited about learning about these animals for the first time. But soon, she became sad after she realized that these animals were endangered. What animals did she learn about? Why are they endangered?

Contents

Amazing Animals of the Amazon

Amazing Animals
of the Amazon

Welcome to Brazil

Mariana Lopes is twelve years old and lives in Brazil.

Brazil is the largest country in South America and is known for the Amazon Rainforest. The rainforests, coastal forests, and palm savannas of the Amazon River basin are home to millions of species of animals and plants.

Mariana gets to visit the forests during her school breaks. Her parents are scientists who study animals. Amazon researchers study animals to learn their habits and how to protect them.

The Amazon Rainforest is in danger.

The trees and brush of the forest provide food and homes for the animals. Because the forests are in danger, the animals living there are also in danger.

KEY WORDS

- be known for
- rainforest
- coastal
- forest
- palm
- savanna
- basin
- home
- species
- researcher
- habit
- protect
- in danger
- brush

During this school break, Mariana is extra lucky.
She will go with her mother to observe giant river otters for one day. Giant river otters are the largest of the thirteen otter species in the world. 

On another day, Mariana will observe lowland tapirs with her father. Lowland tapirs are very sensitive to changes in their habitat and look like small ponies when they run.

▲ giant river otter

▼ lowland tapir

Some friends of her parents will also take Mariana to see hyacinth macaws and golden lion tamarins. Golden lion tamarins, one of the smallest primates in the world, are also one of the most critically endangered animals of the Amazon.

▲ golden lion tamarin

▲ hyacinth macaw

Hyacinth macaws are bright blue birds with gold feathers around their eyes.

Come along with Mariana and learn about some amazing animals of the Amazon.

KEY WORDS

- primate
- critically
- endangered
- come along

Giant River Otters

Mariana leaves her house while it's still dark.

"Mom, why do we have to leave so early? The sun isn't even up yet."

"We have to arrive in the forest before the giant river otters awake," Mom explains. (Aha!)

Mariana's mother studies giant river otters, mammals as comfortable in the water as they are on the ground.

Mariana and her mother stay in the boat and train their eyes and binoculars on a tangle of tree roots on the shore.

▲ giant river otter

Why does Mariana have to leave home while it's still dark?

ⓐ to keep the otters from seeing her
ⓑ to arrive in the forest before the otters wake up

KEY WORDS

- leave
- still
- mammal
- comfortable

- train binoculars on
- tangle
- root
- shore

They are watching the entrance to the den of a family of otters her mother observed yesterday. 

"I left some twigs in front of the opening of their den," her mother explains, "so we can see if they are still there this morning."

A 50-square-meter area around the den has trampled surface vegetation and has been cleared of twigs and debris.

"Otters always clear the debris away from each new den they build," Mariana's mother says.

As the sun rises, a long weasel-like animal comes through the hole between the tangled tree roots. At two meters long, the giant river otter is the largest otter species in the world.

This otter has a white spot on its throat.

KEY WORDS

- entrance
- den
- family
- twig
- in front of
- opening
- square-meter
- trample
- surface vegetation
- be cleared of
- debris
- **rise** (rise-rose-risen)
- weasel
- spot

"Every giant river otter has a different marking on its throat.
A unique mark, like a fingerprint," her mother says. "See?"
Three more otters come out of the den, and each one has
a different marking. One has three white stripes. One has a
small irregular creamy patch. The last one has a diagonal
slash of white on its gray-brown chest.
Another three otters, each with their own distinct throat
marking, join the four on the riverbank.
Together, the seven otters walk to the water and splash in.

"An otter family is called a holt," Mom says. "All members
of the holt do everything together. They hunt, swim, groom,
eat, and sleep together."

Some of the otters glance at their boat.

"They're coming this way," Mariana says excitedly.

"Yes, I've been studying this family for months.  They are
used to me," her mother says.

The biggest otters stay back, but the younger ones swim
right up to the boat and make snorting and whistling noises.

KEY WORDS

- marking
- fingerprint
- out of
- irregular (↔ regular)
- creamy
- patch
- diagonal
- slash
- distinct
- riverbank
- splash
- holt
- groom
- glance
- be used to
- stay back
- snorting
- whistling

"Are they talking to us?" Mariana asks.

"They are probably speaking to each other," Mom explains.
"Giant river otters make nine different sounds, which is
more than any other otter species. They also chirp like birds,
bark like dogs, and roar like lions. Some are clearly warning
sounds and can be heard hundreds of meters away."
The otters splash and swim near the boat for a few more
minutes.

KEY WORDS

- chirp
- bark
- roar
- clearly
- adult
- entire
- surfing
- pop up
- glue
- sleek
- periscope
- submarine

When one of the adults whistles, the others swim toward it.
 The entire holt swims up the river in a way that looks like surfing.

"You see how when they stop swimming, they pop up out of the water and look around?" her mother asks.

Mariana nods, her eyes glued to the sleek animals.

"We call that periscoping. They pop up out of the water like the periscope on a submarine," Mom explains.

Her mother starts the motor on the boat and follows the otters.

The holt soon stops and sits on a log overhanging the slow-moving river.

The otter with the slash across his throat dives under water and comes up with a fish dangling from his mouth. He tears into it with his teeth.

One of the younger otters grunts and tries to steal a bite of fish. The otter with the slash climbs onto the log and continues eating. When he eats his fill, he drops the rest of the fish on the log and lets his younger sibling have it.

After eating, the otters line up on the log, and each one grooms the otter next to him or her.

After grooming, the otters nap in the sun.

"Have you seen enough?" Mom asks.

Mariana shakes her head. "I could watch them all day. They're fun."

"They are fun, and that's one of the reasons they are endangered. People want them as pets or want their sleek fur," her mother says.

"People want their fur? That's terrible," Mariana says.

"Yes, and there are other reasons giant river otters are endangered," her mother says. "Gold mining in the rivers of the rainforest ecosystem uses a chemical called mercury. Mercury poisons the fish otters eat, which, in turn, poisons the otters."

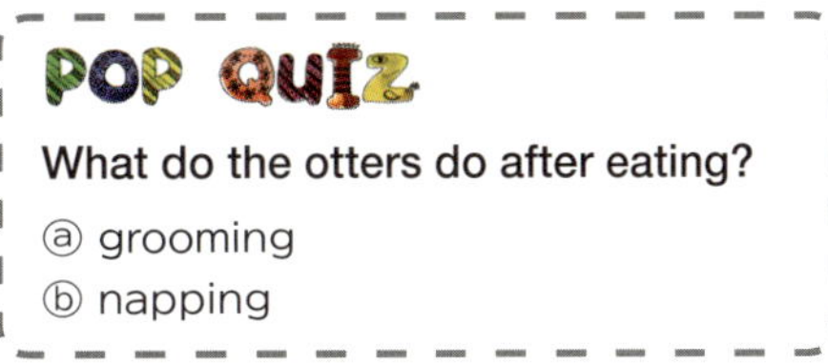

KEY WORDS

- log
- overhang
- dangle
- tear
- grunt
- **steal** (steal-stole-stolen)
- a bite of
- eat one's fill
- rest
- sibling
- line up
- nap
- gold mining
- ecosystem
- chemical
- mercury
- poison
- in turn

"Oh, the poor otters," Mariana says.

"In addition, the forest gets cut down to clear the land for farming and for wood to build houses," her mother continues.

Mariana had never thought about where the wood for houses comes from.

"Giant river otters have no natural predators," Mom says.

"What is a predator?" Mariana asks.

"A predator is an animal that hunts another animal for food," her mother says.

Mariana learned about the food chain in school. 

"Otters are at the top of the food chain here, and no other animal hunts them. However, they are still one of the most endangered mammals in the Amazon."

Her mother shakes her head.

Mariana will learn over the coming days that there are more animals here to protect.

KEY WORDS

- in addition
- clear
- never
- predator
- over
- coming days

Chapter One — Comprehension Quiz

A Choose all the words or phrases that describe giant river otters.

a) 2 meters long

b) feathers

c) sleek fur

d) weasel-like

e) horns

f) rough skin

B Mark T for true or F for false.

❶ An otter's throat marking is as unique as a fingerprint. `T` `F`

❷ Otters approach Mariana's boat because they are familiar with her mother. `T` `F`

❸ A younger otter tries to steal time with the mother otter. `T` `F`

❹ Giant river otters are one of the least endangered mammals in the Amazon. `T` `F`

❺ The giant river otter is the largest otter species in the world. `T` `F`

C

Choose the best answer to each question.

❶ How many sounds do giant river otters make?

a) three   b) seven

c) nine   d) ten

❷ How does Mariana know the otters are friendly?

a) They swim up to the boat and make noises.

b) They stay on the shore and stare at her.

c) They sing to her.

d) They ignore her.

D

Fill in each blank with the right word below.

surfing	nap	debris	top

❶ Giant river otters are at the _______________ of the food chain.

❷ The ground in front of the otter's den has been cleared of twigs and _______________ .

❸ After grooming, the otters _______________ in the sun.

❹ The entire holt swims up the river in a way that looks like they are _______________ .

Lowland Tapirs

Mariana makes another early morning trip into the forest and spends the day with her father. This time, they are following signs to find a very different animal than otters.

While giant river otters are big, lowland tapirs are huge.  They weigh around 300 kilograms!

"We'll have an unusual day today, Mariana," her father says as he searches the ground and surrounding vines for signs that a tapir passed by recently.

▲ lowland tapir

KEY WORDS

- **spend** (spend-spent-spent)
- **unusual** (↔ usual)
- **surrounding**
- **vine**
- **pass by**

Tapirs have a running style like small ponies, and their tough skin protects them from scratching vines. They crash through the branches when running away from predators like jaguars.

"Why, Dad?" she asks.

"Tapirs are not diurnal, meaning active during the day. Tapirs aren't nocturnal either, meaning awake only at night."

Mariana is confused. She thought all animals were either diurnal or nocturnal.

KEY WORDS

- scratch
- crash through
- run away (run-ran-run)
- diurnal
- active
- nocturnal
- either
- confused

"Tapirs are most active at dusk, when it's cooler in the forest. They sleep during the hot day and spend most of the night searching for food," her father explains. 

Mariana has experienced the heat and humidity of the forest in the middle of the day. She knows tapirs are smart to sleep all day.

"Why do you keep stopping to touch the vines?" Mariana asks.

POP QUIZ

When it gets too hot, what do tapirs do?

ⓐ swim
ⓑ sleep

KEY WORDS

- dusk
- experience
- humidity
- in the middle of

"If a tapir ran through here to escape a jaguar, it will have broken some branches and vines. We can follow the path of broken plants until we find a tapir or its most recent nest," her father answers.

"Like hide-and-seek?"

Mariana's father gives a low laugh. "Yes. Tapirs are very shy animals. They are not social like river otters. And a mother tapir will hide her baby in the brush while she searches for fruit to eat until the baby grows big enough to find its own food." 

POP QUIZ

Mark T for true or F for false.

Tapirs and river otters are very shy animals.   T / F

KEY WORDS

- through
- escape
- hide-and-seek
- give a laugh
- social
- enough

"What do tapirs eat?"

"Mangoes or whatever fruit is in season. This forest is also full of different species of palm trees, and tapirs eat the nuts," Mariana's father explains.

They continue walking in silence for a long time. Mariana is getting more and more tired. 

Even though the sun hasn't yet risen, Mariana is sweating from the heat.

"Will we ever find them?" she asks.

Her father stops, and they each sip from a canteen of water.

POP QUIZ

What do tapirs eat?
ⓐ fruits
ⓑ leaves

KEY WORDS

- whatever
- in season
- nut
- in silence

- even though
- sweat
- from the heat
- sip

- canteen
- cool off
- avoid
- by + *Verb*-ing

"I hope so, but, as I said, tapirs are shy. They don't want to be found. Maybe we should head toward the river."

"Why?"

"Because tapirs love to swim," Mariana's father says.

"They swim even though they are big land mammals?" Mariana asks.

Her father nods. "Yes, like hippos in Africa. Tapirs cool off in the water and avoid jaguars by swimming away from them."

Swarms of tiny insects buzz around Mariana's face. She hopes she and her father will find some tapirs soon. She hopes the hot, humid, buggy hike in the rainforest will be worth how tired she is.

Just as she is about to drop to the ground in exhaustion, they arrive at the river.

Her father gestures for her to be quiet and to stay hidden in the brush.

Nearby, a large animal that looks like a cross between a hippo, a horse, and a pig comes out of the water. It is covered in short, coarse brown hair and has a snout like a pig.

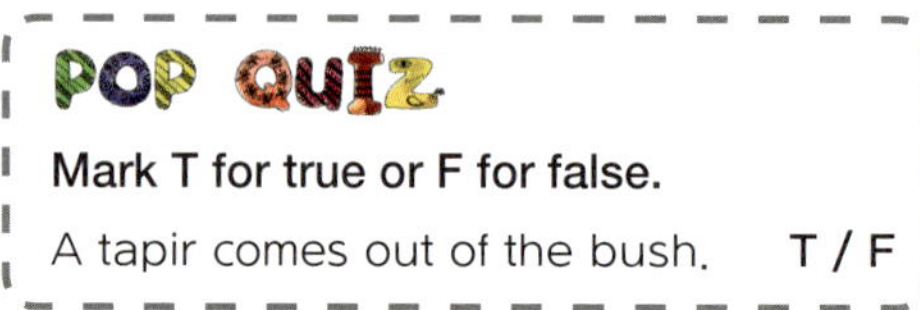

KEY WORDS

- swarm
- buzz
- humid
- buggy
- hike
- worth
- be about to

- in exhaustion
- gesture
- stay hidden
- nearby
- a cross between
- coarse
- snout

As she watches, the tapir uses its snout to grab a mango from a high branch. It brings the mango into some brush. Looking carefully, Mariana notices another animal among the grass and bushes.  This animal is smaller and reddish-brown with rows of white spots that are almost like stripes.

KEY WORDS

- grab
- reddish-brown
- row

A baby tapir!

"The baby's fur is a different
color, so it can stay hidden
more easily in the forest,"
Mariana's father explains.
"As it grows up, it will
lose the spots and start to
look more and more like its
mother."

Mariana nods. She learned about
camouflage in school. Lots of
animals use camouflage to hide
from predators by blending into their surroundings.

▲ baby tapir

KEY WORDS
- **grow up** (grow-grew-grown)
- **camouflage**
- **blend into**

"Tapirs are mammals like humans, jaguars, and monkeys,"
Dad explains.  "This means that the mother gives birth to
a live animal. That's unlike birds and reptiles, which lay eggs
that eventually hatch."

Mariana has seen lots of birds' nests with eggs.

"Tapirs do not lay eggs," her dad says. "They give birth to
live baby tapirs."

A baby tapir is in front of Mariana now.

"Another interesting thing about tapirs is that babies are not
born until they are big enough to walk on their own," Dad
says. "Could you walk when you were born?"

Her eyes wide, Mariana shakes her head. Human babies
need many months to grow before they can walk.

▲ one of mammals

KEY WORDS

- **give birth to** (give-gave-given)
- **unlike** (↔ like)
- **reptile**
- **lay** (lay-laid-laid)
- **eventually**
- **hatch**
- **be born**
- **on one's own**

Soon, the tapirs lumber away, probably to go to their nests to sleep as the sun begins to rise above the horizon.

"Time to go," Mariana's father says.

"Already?" Mariana pouts. She loves watching the animals in the forest. This visit to the rainforest was too short.

"It's going to get hot," Dad says. "We will go to my office for a while. I will write up some notes on our observations from today."

"Did you learn anything new?" Mariana asks. 

"I keep track of everything I witness in the forest," Dad says.

"You never know what piece of information will help."

Mariana nods.

"You can rest and have a cold drink," Dad continues.

"We will return before sunset when the tapirs are active again."

▲ a sleeping tapir

KEY WORDS

- keep track of
- witness
- return
- sunset

Several hours later, Mariana and her father return to the
forest. She is rested and refreshed. The air is cooler now.
Dad leads her to a muddy spot where the mostly flat ground
is littered with twigs and fronds.

"Where are we?" Mariana asks.

"This is a salt lick," Dad answers.

"What is a salt lick?" she asks.

She doesn't see any salt around. She only sees the trampled
plants on the ground and the tall, skinny trees looming above
them.

"A salt lick is also called a clay lick," her father explains.

"It is a spot like this."

He gestures around them.

"The ground here is made up of wet clay that is rich in salt." Aha!

Mariana makes a face. Why did her father bring her to see salty mud?

"Salt has minerals the animals need and can't get from fruits, nuts, and seeds," he says.

"Do tapirs need to lick salt?" she asks.

"Yes. Tapirs visit the salt lick every day," her father says.

"In fact, dozens of species visit this salt lick."

"Really? What other species?" Mariana asks.

KEY WORDS

- rested
- refreshed
- muddy
- be littered with
- frond

- salt lick
- skinny
- looming
- be made up of
- rich in

- make a face
- mineral
- lick
- dozens of

▲ jaguar

▲ ocelot

▲ anteater

▲ howler monkey

▲ brocket deer

▲ peccary

▲ armadillo

"Jaguars, ocelots, anteaters, howler monkeys, great brocket deer, peccaries, and giant armadillos." Mariana's father counts them off on his fingers.

Despite the heat, Mariana shivers. "Jaguars and ocelots? Those are fast, large cats. They are dangerous."

"That is true," Dad agrees. "They hunt at night, so we will leave here soon before it gets dark."

They back up into the surrounding forest while hoping that some animals will come to the salt lick.

KEY WORDS

- count them off on one's fingers
- despite
- shiver

- cat
- back up

After an hour, the air is even cooler and beginning to get dark.

"We had better go," Dad says. "The animals must smell us, so they are not approaching."

Mariana nods. She does not want to stay in the forest after dark. She doesn't want to meet a hungry jaguar.

On the way home, Mariana asks her father a question that has bothered her all day. "Why do you need to study the tapirs, Dad?"

"Tapirs are one of the biggest mammals in the forest. They are sensitive to changes in their environment, which is why their status is vulnerable. They don't survive well when their habitat is in danger."

Mariana pouts again. She wants the tapirs to be safe in their forest.

"As tapirs eat fruit," her father continues, "they leave the seeds behind, and they grow into new plants and trees. If we don't learn to protect tapirs, the forest won't keep growing."

Mariana nods.

"Without the forest, lots of other animals and birds will have no source of food and nowhere to live," he says. "They will all die out."

Mariana doesn't want Amazon animals like otters and tapirs to become extinct. "You have to save them, Dad!"

Mariana's father nods. "I know, my sweet girl. I'm trying."

Mark T for true or F for false.

Tapirs are vulnerable because the forest is in danger.   T / F

KEY WORDS

- approach
- bother
- status

- vulnerable
- survive
- source

- die out
- extinct
- sweet

Comprehension Quiz

A Choose all the features of lowland tapirs.

a) They weigh 100 kilograms.

b) They love to swim.

c) They are only awake at night.

d) They are give birth to babies.

B Mark T for true or F for false.

❶ Tapirs are social animals like otters.   T   F

❷ A baby tapir's camouflage coloring keeps the baby
in the brush hidden from predators.   T   F

❸ Mariana sees salt in the salt lick.   T   F

❹ Amazon animals visit salt licks because they like the
taste of salt.   T   F

❺ A salt lick is also called a mineral bath.   T   F

 Choose the best answer to each question.

1 What animals do tapirs run like?

a) ponies   b) hippos

c) cats   d) dogs

2 Why does the rainforest need tapirs?

a) They keep the population of jaguars down.

b) They spread the seeds of the fruits they eat.

c) They knock down trees to make room for other animals.

d) They eat poisonous plants.

D Choose the right phrase for each blank.

1 Mariana and her father first enter the forest _____________.

a) at noon

b) in the early morning

c) at night

d) in the late afternoon

2 The tapir uses _____________ to grab the mango.

a) its legs   b) its horn

c) its snout   d) a hook

Golden Lion Tamarins

The next time Mariana wakes up before dawn, she travels into the rainforest with her father's friend Rafael Oliveira. Rafael studies golden lion tamarins, which are members of the primate family. Monkeys, chimpanzees, and gorillas are also primates.

Golden lion tamarins are also called golden marmosets. Marmosets are another family of monkeys.

"We arrive this early to observe the early morning rituals of tamarins," Rafael tells Mariana.

Rafael and Mariana drive into the Poço das Antas biological reserve in the Brazilian state of Rio. Next, they ride on a boat on a slow-moving river. Mariana is tired and nervous but excited to see the animals Rafael spends all his time studying. Eventually, they reach a dock. Mariana steps into a thick forest filled with woody vines and bright tropical flowering plants.

"To see the tamarins, you have to look up," Rafael says.

KEY WORDS

- dawn
- ritual
- tell (tell-told-told)
- biological
- reserve
- nervous
- dock
- woody
- tropical

They walk deep into the forest while brushing past scratchy
vines.

Mariana tries to look up, but she also has to watch where
she puts her feet.

Rafael and Mariana climb up to a wooden deck built between
the branches of a tree. 

"From up here, we'll be able to watch the golden lion
tamarins," Rafael says. "This is called the sub canopy
because it's underneath the canopy of the leaves. The leaves
block the view of predators and some of the heat of the sun."

POP QUIZ

Where is the wooden deck?
ⓐ between the branches of a tree
ⓑ in the hole of a tree

KEY WORDS

- brush past
- scratchy
- deck
- **build** (build-built-built)
- from up

- **be able to** (= can)
- sub
- canopy
- underneath
- view

"Which animals hunt tamarins?" Mariana asks.

"Jaguars, large snakes, weasels, and hunting birds such as eagles and hawks," Rafael answers.

Soon, Mariana hears a loud animal call.

She looks across the vines and sees a tiny face surrounded by golden hair coming out of a hole in a tree. Aha!

A monkey about the size of a squirrel with a tail around 30 centimeters long looks at Mariana and Rafael.

KEY WORDS

- hawk
- surrounded by
- squirrel

"Oh no, he saw us," she says. "Will he leave now?"

"No, he will warn the others. Then, he will wait and see what we do. Sit very still," Rafael says.

Mariana sits still and watches.

The monkey screeches back into the nest.

Despite the sound, Mariana thinks he looks just like a miniature lion.

The tiny golden monkey stares at the two humans for several minutes.

"Adult golden lion tamarins weigh less than 700 grams," Rafael explains.

They are smaller than some of the flowers growing above Mariana's head.

What kinds of noises do tamarins make to warn others?

ⓐ screeches
ⓑ cackles

KEY WORDS

- warn
- screech
- miniature
- stare at
- less
- than

Mariana doesn't think she can stay still any longer when the tamarin sends a different screech into the tree.

The first tamarin is soon joined by three others. High-pitched whistles and screeches pierce the air.

Mariana is tempted to cover her ears, but she's delighted by the noise coming from such small bodies.

Two of the newcomers are even smaller than the original tamarin.

"Those are the babies," Rafael points out. "They are twins. Golden lion tamarin mothers usually give birth to twins."

The tamarins sip water out of a nearby flower. Next, they jump from branch to branch until they reach some fruit growing far above the ground. They share the fruit.

▲ a golden lion tamarin with a baby

The tiny creatures continue to run across branches and between vines. Mariana keeps watching them through binoculars.

The tamarins go to the end of a branch. The next branch is five meters away.

"Oh no, Rafael," Mariana says in a loud whisper. "It's too far."

"Shh. Just watch."

POP QUIZ

Why do the tamarins jump across the wide space?
ⓐ to find food
ⓑ to avoid the hunters

KEY WORDS

- from A to B
- share
- to the end of
- whisper

The tamarins easily jump across the wide space and continue searching for fruit.

Mariana's heart pounds. She wishes she could jump that far.

After eating, the tamarins rest during the hottest part of the day.

Mariana wishes to nap, too. The thick canopy of leaves far above her head blocks the sun, but the forest is still hot and humid.

Between naps, the tamarins groom each other. Long fingers pluck through tangles in their lion-colored fur. When they get hungry again, the monkeys turn their efforts to finding insects.

KEY WORDS

- space
- pound
- pluck
- turn one's efforts to

Although a long day, Mariana is surprised when Rafael gestures to her to climb down the ladder. She could watch the acrobatic golden primates all day!

"Can't we please stay?" she asks.

Rafael smiles. "I know how fun and cute they are, but we need to leave the forest before night falls. We don't want to face the same predators the tamarins do."

Mariana remembers her father warning her about jaguars and ocelots.

Mariana knows that jaguars are the third biggest cats in the world and the largest cats in the Americas. They can climb trees and swim.

KEY WORDS

- surprised
- acrobatic
- night falls
- face
- jaw

- prey
- fierce
- similar
- **hang out** (hang-hung-hung)
- rodent

A jaguar's powerful jaws can kill its prey in one bite. Mariana shivers in fear.

An ocelot is smaller than a jaguar, but it is bigger than a house cat.

Ocelots are just as fierce and dangerous as jaguars. They look similar, with yellow skin and black markings. Ocelots often hang out in trees.

Luckily for Mariana and Rafael, ocelots hunt for animals much smaller than themselves. They eat lizards, frogs, crabs, rodents, and rabbits. Aha!

▲ jaguar

▲ ocelot

"Why do you study tamarins, Rafael?" Mariana asks on the way home.

"Because their habitat—where they live—is becoming smaller," Rafael answers.

"Smaller? How?" Mariana asks. The forest she visited today was so much bigger than anything she could imagine.

"Trees are being cut down so that people can farm or use the wood to build houses," Rafael explains.

That is what Mariana's mother told her the other day.

"So there is less forest for the tamarins to live in," Rafael continues. "There are just small bits of forest that are no longer connected to each other. Tamarins can't travel between the small bits of forest, so they have smaller areas in which to find food."

POP QUIZ

Mark T for true or F for false.

One problem facing the habitat of tamarins is that trees get cut down.   T / F

KEY WORDS

- imagine
- so that
- the other day

- bit
- connect
- someday

- decide
- so far

These are some of the same problems Mariana's father and
mother told her about earlier in the week. All of the Amazon
species are vulnerable or in danger for similar reasons.
Mariana loves watching the otters play, the tamarins jump,
and the tapirs eat fruit. She hopes to visit them all again
someday.
Mariana decides that she'd like to be a researcher someday,
too, so that she can learn to protect the Amazon Rainforest
for all the animals she has visited so far.

Comprehension Quiz

A Look at the picture and fill in each blank.

A golden lion tamarin is a tiny

_______________ with

_______________ hair and a

_______________ tail.

B Mark T for true or F for false.

❶ Mariana watches the tamarins from the ground.   T   F

❷ Adult tamarins are smaller than some flowers
growing above Mariana's head.   T   F

❸ Tamarins sip water from flowers.   T   F

❹ Jaguars are the largest cats in the world.   T   F

❺ Ocelots hang out in trees.   T   F

C Choose the best answer to each question.

❶ When the first tamarin sees Mariana and Rafael, what does he do?

a) He goes over to greet them.

b) He yells and runs away.

c) He warns his family and watches them.

d) He goes back into the tree.

❷ What word best describes the tamarins?

a) lazy   b) fearful

c) acrobatic   d) shy

D Put the sentences in order.

❶ Golden lion tamarins jump from branch to branch until they reach some fruit growing far above the ground.

❷ The tiny golden monkey stares at the two humans for several minutes.

❸ Rafael and Mariana drive into the Poço das Antas biological reserve in the Brazilian state of Rio.

❹ Mariana sees a tiny face surrounded by golden hair coming out of a hole in a tree.

_______ → _______ → _______ → _______

Hyacinth Macaws

Mariana stares at a huge tree so tall that she has to shade her eyes from the sun to see the leaves. Like on the day with Rafael, Mariana perches on a wooden deck among the trees. This time, she visits a palm savanna with Fernanda Alves, another friend of her parents.

Fernanda is a scientist who studies birds.

Now, Fernanda points to a hole in the trunk of the tall tree.

"A hyacinth macaw has built a nest in this tree," Fernanda says. 

She hands a pair of binoculars to Mariana.

"This kind of tree is old enough and wide enough for a nest," Fernanda says. "Macaws can hollow out the soft wood with their beak."

"How can you tell there is a nest there?" Mariana asks. She only sees a dark spot on the trunk, not a nest.

"Watch."

In a few minutes, movement catches Mariana's eye. Bright blue feathers appear, and Mariana picks out a pointy beak and eyes surrounded by gold.

POP QUIZ

What does Fernanda study?
ⓐ birds
ⓑ reptiles

KEY WORDS

- shade
- perch on
- trunk
- hand
- a pair of
- hollow out
- beak
- appear
- pick out
- pointy

"There it is!" she shouts, too excited to stay quiet. 

The bird is about one meter long.

"Hyacinth macaws are the largest parrots in the world," Fernanda says. "They prefer lightly forested grasslands like this instead of the rainforest."

The bird flies to a palm tree and gathers nuts, and then it brings them back to its nest in the tree.

"This must be the father macaw," Fernanda says. "The father goes out looking for food to bring back to the babies resting in the nest with the mother."

KEY WORDS

- lightly
- forested
- grassland
- unripe (↔ ripe)
- poisonous
- digest
- chunk
- absorb

Fernanda hands the pair of binoculars back to Mariana. Mariana watches the bright blue bird fly further away to collect an unripe mango.

"They eat it before it's ripe?" she asks.

Fernanda nods. "They also eat seeds poisonous to other species. We believe macaws are able to digest fruits and seeds dangerous to other animals because macaws also eat clay from riverbanks."

"How does the clay help?" Mariana asks.

"We're not sure, but we think the chunks of clay macaws eat must absorb the poisons," Fernanda explains.

Choose the correct word.

The hyacinth macaw lives in the (ⓐ rainforest / ⓑ palm savanna).

Macaws eat clay, and tapirs eat salt.

Mariana realizes that some animals have strange eating habits.

"Macaws serve an important function in the forest," Fernanda says.

"As they eat fruits and nuts, they disperse seeds all over the savanna that will someday grow into more trees. So macaws help regenerate their own habitat." 

Mariana thinks that is just like the lowland tapirs!

Fernanda leads Mariana to a different wooden deck.

She wants Mariana to see an entire flock of hyacinth macaws.

POP QUIZ

Choose the correct word.

Macaws distribute seeds from the fruits they eat just like (ⓐ tapirs / ⓑ jaguars).

KEY WORDS

- realize
- eating habit
- serve
- function
- disperse
- all over
- regenerate
- flock

▲ termite mound

On the way, Fernanda points out a pointy and irregular hill of dirt erupting from the ground.

"That is a termite mound," Fernanda says. Aha!

Eww, termites.

"Where there are termites, there are giant armadillos," Fernanda says.

"I know armadillos have a bony shell that looks like armor," Mariana says. "The skin underneath is scaly."

"Yes, that is true," agrees Fernanda.

▲ armadillo

"But what is a giant armadillo?" Mariana asks.

"As the name implies, the giant armadillo is a much larger species," Fernanda explains.  "It can grow to a meter and a half in length. It can weigh up to 58 kilograms."

"That's big. What else do they eat?" Mariana asks.

"They also eat ants." Fernanda keeps walking through the forest. "They have strong legs and sharp claws to reach even the tallest termite mounds."

"They must be difficult to hunt with claws and a shell," Mariana says.

"They are hunted by jaguars and pumas," Fernanda says. "And like so many other animals in the Amazon, giant armadillos are endangered."

KEY WORDS

- imply
- claw
- announce
- platform
- lose count (lose-lost-lost)
- wheel
- squawk

Mariana is sad to hear how many species in her country are
endangered.

"Here we are," Fernanda announces. "Climb up."

When they arrive at the new platform, Mariana counts
eighteen bright blue macaws before losing count.

The birds fly from branch to branch, wheel around under the
canopy, and squawk and scream.

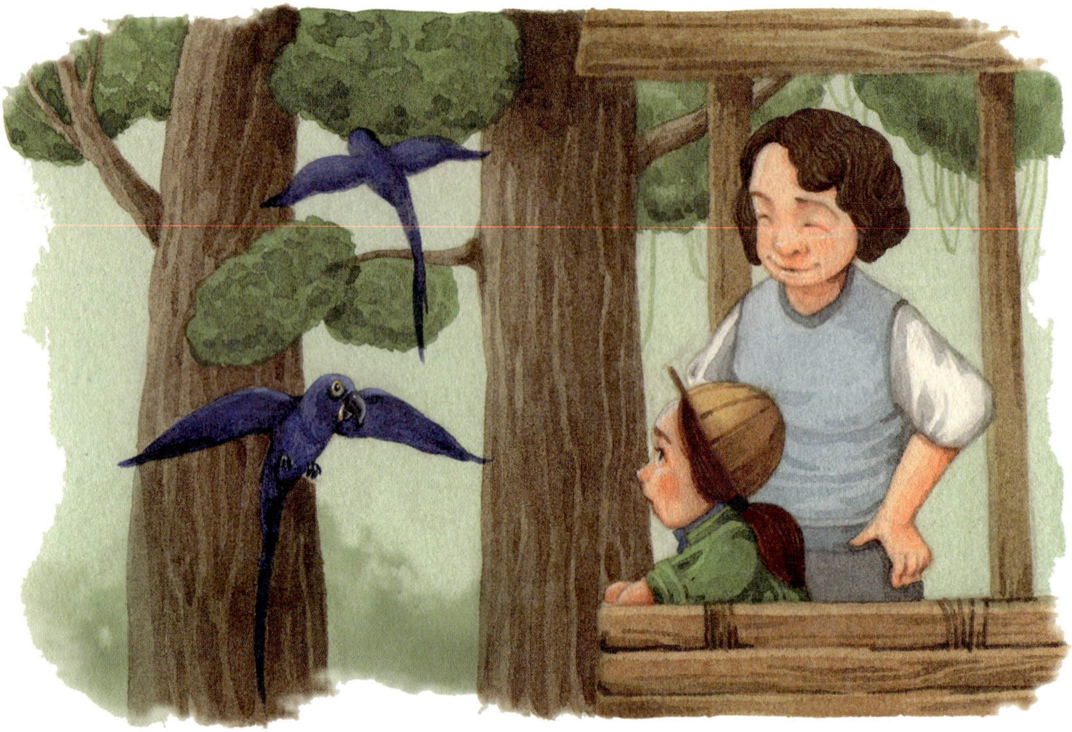

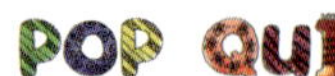

"It sounds like they're yelling at each other," Mariana says. "Macaws make a few different sounds to mark their territory and to identify members of their flock," Fernanda says. Aha! Even while watching the macaws in awe, Mariana thinks about all the animals she visited during this week of school vacation.

POP QUIZ

Why do macaws make a few different sounds?

ⓐ to mark their territory
ⓑ to disperse seeds

"Are hyacinth macaws endangered, too?" she asks Fernanda.
Fernanda nods. "Yes, macaws are endangered. Just like with
otters, tapirs, and tamarins, one of the biggest reasons is
habitat loss."

Mariana nods. The reasons are becoming familiar.
"Mechanized agriculture, cattle ranching, and hydroelectric
power all require land cleared of trees and brush," Fernanda
says. "Without the trees and brush, the land isn't fit for
the species you have observed."

▲ hydroelectric dam

KEY WORDS

- mark one's territory
- identify
- in awe
- loss
- familiar
- mechanized

- agriculture
- cattle ranching
- hydroelectric power
- require
- fit for

Mariana realizes that hyacinth macaws are pretty birds with their bright blue and gold feathers. "I bet people would like to have macaws as pets, too."

"Yes, which is why buying and selling endangered animals is illegal. The laws don't stop everyone, however." Fernanda hands a canteen to Mariana.

Mariana takes a long drink. The heat makes her thirsty.

"Another problem for macaws is the feather art made by local Indians," Fernanda says. "Tourists love the beautiful artwork and are willing to pay a lot of money for it."

"What is feather art?" Mariana asks.

KEY WORDS

- illegal (↔ legal)
- take a long drink
- local
- Indian
- tourist
- artwork
- be willing to
- population
- involve
- costume
- headdress
- be made from
- snakeskin
- casing
- fiber

"Local Indian populations in the Amazon had rituals that often involved costumes, masks, and headdresses. These costumes were made from feathers, snakeskin, bark, insect casings, plant fibers, and seeds," Fernanda explains.

"Those are a lot of materials," Mariana says.

"Feathers from many species of birds and of all colors are important to their costumes," Fernanda continues.

"What a lot of poor birds," Mariana thinks.

"Headdresses were made by weaving the different materials together," Fernanda tells her. "They are tied around a person's head for a particular ritual."

"What kind of rituals?" Mariana asks.

"Coming-of-age ceremonies, baby-naming ceremonies, weddings, and funerals. Such events are popular in many cultures," Fernanda says. "In addition, shamans—native healers—wore full body costumes made of feathers and plant fibers during healing rituals."

"Healing rituals?" Mariana frowns.

"Yes. Now, we have doctors and medicines to cure those who are sick or injured. Ancient cultures used items from nature to make people better," Fernanda explains. "Herbs, seeds, and rituals."

KEY WORDS

- weave
- tie
- coming-of-age
- ceremony

- baby-naming
- funeral
- popular
- shaman

- healer
- wear (wear-wore-worn)
- healing
- ancient

"Can't they make art with feathers that fall off naturally?"
Mariana asks.

Fernanda smiles. "Yes, and that is what we are trying to
teach people. We suggest they use fallen feathers instead of
trapping and killing the birds first."

Mariana looks thoughtful. It has been an amazing week in
the rainforest. She hopes she can visit again soon.

KEY WORDS

- trap
- thoughtful

Saving the Animals

Mariana arrives home tired yet again. She can't stop thinking about Amazon animals. She wants to help them but doesn't know how.

Over dinner with her parents, she learns that researchers encourage ranchers to leave trees with macaw nests alone. They plant more food trees and convince governments to enforce local protection laws.

Some scientists create artificial nests to give the macaws more places to live.

Mariana remembers how friendly and playful the otters were.

"That's why tourists pay to visit the giant river otters," Dad explains.

Mariana understands why people would want to watch the otters play. They were so fun!

"The government needs to create more protected areas for otters. All tourism projects must respect the needs of otters," Mom says.

KEY WORDS

- yet again
- encourage
- rancher
- convince
- enforce
- artificial
- playful
- tourism
- needs

Mariana nods. Tourists would also love the social golden lion tamarins.

"Planting trees is one of the most important things we can do for the animals," Mariana's mother says. "New trees will keep the forest from shrinking and make sure the animals have food and shelter."

"Some macaws and tamarins born in zoos around the world are brought to the Amazon to increase their populations," Mariana's father says.

"Animals in zoos around the world can save the animals here in Brazil?" Mariana asks.

"Yes," her mother agrees.

"The Poço das Antas biological reserve you visited this week was created to preserve the tamarins' habitat," Mom says.

KEY WORDS

- keep from
- shrink (shrink-shrank-shrunk)
- shelter
- preserve
- closed to
- thrive

"The land is closed to visitors. The reserve is only for education and research. Tamarins have thrived there, and the population is growing," her mother explains.

Mariana nods.

Increasing the populations of giant river otters, lowland tapirs, golden lion tamarins, and hyacinth macaws sounds like a good idea.

Mariana will be able to share the animals with her own children one day.

Comprehension Quiz

A Mark T for true or F for false.

❶ The father macaw gathers food for the babies. T F

❷ The macaw eats clay because it tastes good. T F

❸ People in ancient cultures healed sick people by using items from nature. T F

❹ Habitat loss is a major reason animals are endangered. T F

B Choose the best answer to each question.

❶ Where do macaws make their nests?

a) in the sand

b) in tall trees with soft wood

c) in hard trees

d) in the water

❷ Which food does the hyacinth macaw NOT eat?

a) unripe mangoes

b) meat

c) poisonous seeds

d) clay

C Solve the crossword puzzle.

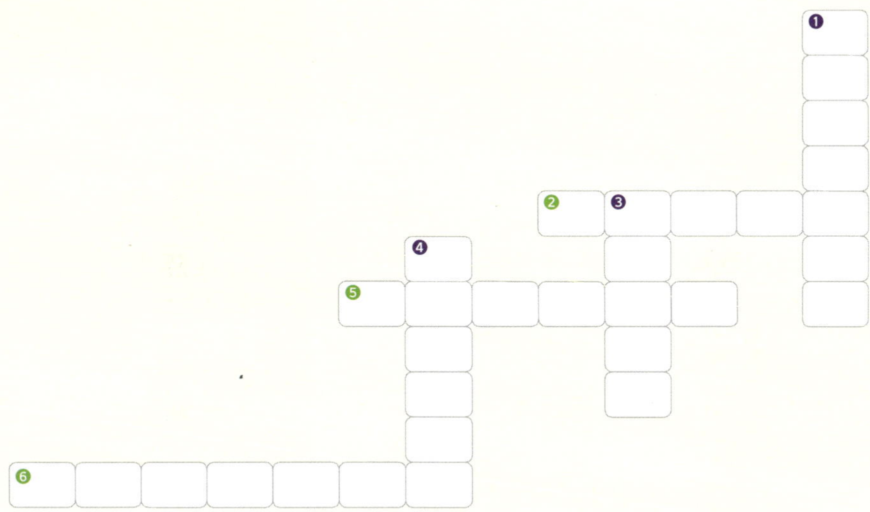

Across

❷ a playful mammal in the Amazon

❺ the umbrella of leaves at the top of the rainforest

❻ an item used in native art

Down

❶ a social monkey that tourists love

❸ an animal that eats salt

❹ an Amazon predator that hunts a giant armadilo

Fill in the blanks to review the story.

❶ Title: __________

❷ Place: __________

❸ Main Point:

Mariana observes four different __________.

❹ Giant River Otters

- mammal comfortable in the __________
- largest otter species in the __________
- each otter has a unique mark on its __________
- an otter __________ is called a holt

❺ Lowland Tapirs

- run like small __________
- love to __________ like hippos
- babies are born big enough to __________
- visit a __________ for minerals

❻ Golden Lion Tamarins

- are a kind of __________
- have __________ fur
- usually give birth to __________
- can easily __________ far

❼ Hyacinth Macaws

- hollow out wood with their __________
- the largest __________ in the world
- the __________ looks for food
- eat __________ and fruit

Let's Think & Talk

Think about the following questions and answer them freely.

❶ Tell us why some animals in the Amazon are endangered.

❷ Tell us what we can do to protect endangered animals.

❸ What animals would you want to see if you went to the Amazon? Why?

❹ Tell us what we can do to protect our environment and animals.

Let's Review the Story

❶ Title: Amazing Animals of the Amazon

❷ Place: Amazon Rainforest

❸ Main Point:
Mariana observes four different **animals**.

❹ Giant River Otters
- mammal comfortable in the **water**
- largest otter species in the **world**
- each otter has a unique mark on its **throat**
- an otter **family** is called a holt

❺ Lowland Tapirs
- run like small **ponies**
- love to **swim** like hippos
- babies are born big enough to **walk**
- visit a **salt lick** for minerals

❻ Golden Lion Tamarins
- are a kind of **monkey**
- have **golden** fur
- usually give birth to **twins**
- can easily **jump** far

❼ Hyacinth Macaws
- hollow out wood with their **beaks**
- the largest **parrots** in the world
- the **father** looks for food
- eat **clay** and fruit

After-reading Test

- **Amazing Animals of the Amazon**
- **Level 5**
- **26 Questions**

  (Vocabulary 5 / Reading Comprehension 16 /

  Sentence Structure & Grammar 5)

1. Which of the following is the wrong past tense form of the verb?
   ① grew
   ② reached
   ③ stealed
   ④ hung

2. Which of the following words has the wrong opposite?
   ① like ↔ unlike
   ② legal ↔ illegal
   ③ regular ↔ irregular
   ④ ripe ↔ irripe

3. Which of the following is similar to the word "habitat"?
   ① holt
   ② home
   ③ flock
   ④ entrance

4. What is the common word for the two blanks?

   - They are used ___________ me.
   - This means that the mother gives birth ___________ a live animal.

   ① on
   ② to
   ③ for
   ④ with

5. What are the proper words for the blanks?

   ① in – for – on
   ② of – to – with
   ③ for – off – of
   ④ with – in – for

6. How many otters make up the family Mariana observes?
   ① five
   ② six
   ③ seven
   ④ eight

7. What chemical is used in gold mining in the Amazon?
   ① oxygen
   ② mercury
   ③ hydrogen
   ④ lead

8. Choose all of the reasons giant river otters are endangered.
   ① They are hunted by big cats.
   ② People hunt them for their sleek fur.
   ③ People trap them for pets.
   ④ Otters are picky eaters.

9. Why do tapirs have tough skin?
    ① to help them swim
    ② to keep them warm
    ③ to protect them from jaguars
    ④ to protect them from scratching vines

10. Why does Mariana's father stop to touch the vines on their way into the
    forest?
    ① to see if a running tapir broke any branches
    ② to check if they are part of a nest
    ③ to see if they are prickly
    ④ to smell a tapir

11. When it gets hot, the tapirs go to sleep. What do Mariana and her father
    do?
    ① They sleep in the forest.
    ② They find a restaurant.
    ③ They rest in her father's office.
    ④ They watch the tapirs sleep.

12. What animal family are tamarins part of?
    ① reptile
    ② primate
    ③ bird
    ④ fish

13. What does Mariana decide to become at the end of the day after observing tamarins?

① a doctor

② an animal trainer

③ an artist

④ an Amazon researcher

14. How do macaws make a nest?

① They burrow in the sand.

② They dig with their claws.

③ They hollow out the wood with their beak.

④ They collect small branches and put them in trees.

15. Which food does the macaw eat?

① unripe mangoes

② meat

③ fish

④ salt

16. Which of the following are NOT kinds of feather art?

① costumes

② masks

③ teapots

④ headdresses

17. Choose all the animals that hunt the giant armadillo.
　① jaguar
　② tamarin
　③ puma
　④ tapir

※ Choose each sentence that does NOT match the story. (18~21)
18. ① The otters splash and swim near the boat.
　② Gold mining poisons the fish the otters eat.
　③ The otters line up on a log, and each one grooms the otter next to him or her.
　④ The youngest otter leaves the holt to hunt on its own.

19. ① Lowland tapirs weigh 200 kilograms.
　② Tapirs love to swim.
　③ The baby tapir has rows of spots on its skin.
　④ Tapirs sleep during the hot day.

20. ① Adult golden lion tamarins weigh fewer than 700 grams.
　② Rafael studies tamarins to protect them.
　③ Golden lion tamarin mothers can't give birth to twins.
　④ The tamarins easily jump across the wide space.

21. ① At one meter long, hyacinth macaws are the largest parrots in the world.
　② Giant armadillos have soft skin.
　③ Giant armadillos eat ants and termites.
　④ Macaws make a few different sounds to mark their territory.

22.
They spend most of the night to search for food.
    ①   ②   ③ ④

23.
The baby grew enough big to find its own food.
    ①   ②   ③   ④

※ Choose the right sentence. (24~25)

24. ① I know how fun and cute they are.
   ② I know how they fun and cute are.
   ③ I know how are they fun and cute.
   ④ I know they are how fun and cute.

25. ① She was to excited too stay quiet.
   ② She was so excited stayed quiet.
   ③ She was too excited stay quiet.
   ④ She was too excited to stay quiet.

26. Which is the right word for the blank?

As the name implies, the giant armadillo is a _________ larger species.

① more   ② most
③ much   ④ best

Memo

Memo

Memo

Memo

Brooke Rousseau
Brooke Rousseau is a writer, mother, and French teacher who strives to make the exotic familiar. Driven by a fascination with other cultures, Brooke has lived in Europe, Africa, and the United States, and visited parts of the Middle East and South America. She has earned degrees in French Literature and International Relations. Brooke writes nonfiction for older elementary children, short stories for very young children, and middle grade and young adult novels.

Amazing Animals of the Amazon

Written by Brooke Rousseau
Illustrated by Jinwoo Kim

First Published in December 2014

Editorial Manager: Juyon Choi
Editors: Kyunghee Jang, Jiyeong Park
Designers: Eunhee Lee, Elim
Cover Designer: Eunhee Lee

Published and distributed by

Darakwon Bldg., 64-1 Jandari-ro, Mapo-gu, Seoul, Korea 121-894
Tel: 82-2-736-2031(ext. 250)   Fax: 82-2-736-2037
Homepage: www.ihappyhouse.co.kr
Publisher: Kyudo Chung

ISBN: 978-89-6653-166-0 18740 / 978-89-6653-156-1 18740(set)

[Components]
• 1 Audio CD (Recording Studio: Aram)
• Answer Keys & Korean Translation: Free download at www.ihappyhouse.co.kr